DISCOVERING GEOGRAPHY

MEASUREMENTS

FRAN SAMMIS

ART BY RICHARD MACCABE

BENCHMARK BOOKS

MARSHALL CAVENDISH
NEW YORK

Benchmark Books
Marshall Cavendish Corporation
99 White Plains Road
Tarrytown, New York 10591

©Marshall Cavendish Corporation, 1998

Series created by Blackbirch Graphics, Inc.

Printed and bound in the United States.

Library of Congress Cataloging-in-Publication Data

Sammis, Fran.
    Measurements / by Fran Sammis.
        p.   cm. — (Discovering geography)
    Includes index.
    Summary: Explains how to measure distance on maps through use of scale bars, color keys, and contour lines; includes suggested activities to illustrate the concepts.
    ISBN 0-7614-0539-9 (lib. bdg.)
    1. Distances—Measurement—Juvenile literature. 2. Map scales—Juvenile literature. [1. Distances. 2. Measurement. 3. Maps.] I. Title. II. Series: Discovering geography (New York, N.Y.)
G109.S26   1998
912'.01'48—dc21

                                                97-383
                                               CIP
                                                  AC

Contents

Pace It Off

On modern maps, measurements such as feet or miles mean the same thing to everyone. This wasn't always true. Long ago, people measured things by comparing them to parts of the body, such as thumbs and feet. People also measured by paces. A pace was the distance covered by a walking step. But since people come in different sizes, getting exact measurements wasn't easy.

Try measuring this way yourself. Step heel-to-toe and count how many "feet" it is:

- from the sidewalk to your front door, or front steps;

- from your bedroom door to your bed.

Have a grown-up do the same thing. Write the results on a piece of paper. What differences did you find?

Next, walk (don't run) those same distances. Count how many paces, or steps, it takes to reach your goal. Have a shorter or taller friend do the same thing. Write down the results. What did you find?

If you drew maps of how far each distance was, would the maps look the same? Why or why not?

4

Large-Scale: Small-Scale

A large-scale map shows a small area close-up. You can show a lot of details on this kind of map. A small-scale map shows a large area in much less detail.

How would these maps be re-ordered if you put them in large-scale to small-scale order?

Things look pretty small from up here—like a small-scale map.

A

North America

B
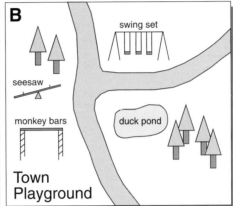
seesaw
monkey bars
swing set
duck pond
Town Playground

C
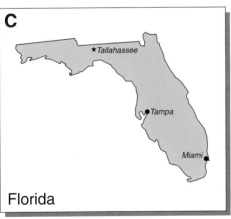
★Tallahassee
●Tampa
Miami●
Florida

D
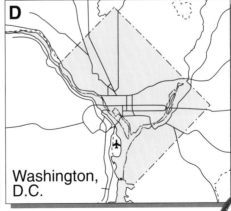
Washington, D.C.

A large-scale map enlarges a place.

Near and Far

Can you tell how far apart places really are by looking on a map? Sure! Just look for the scale bar:

This one tells you that 1 inch on the map equals 3 miles on the ground. Use a ruler and the scale bar on Frontier Fred's Old West map to find these distances:

- How far is it from Snowy Mountain to Secret Canyon?

- Which distance is greater: Midas Mine to Cold Creek Bridge, or Cold Creek Bridge to the Ranch House?

- Which route from Fort Prairie Dog to Armadillo City is shorter: Eagle Alley to Pony Pass, or Coyote Road to Pony Pass?

- How far is it from the Ranch House to Armadillo City?

FRONTIER FRED'S OLD WEST

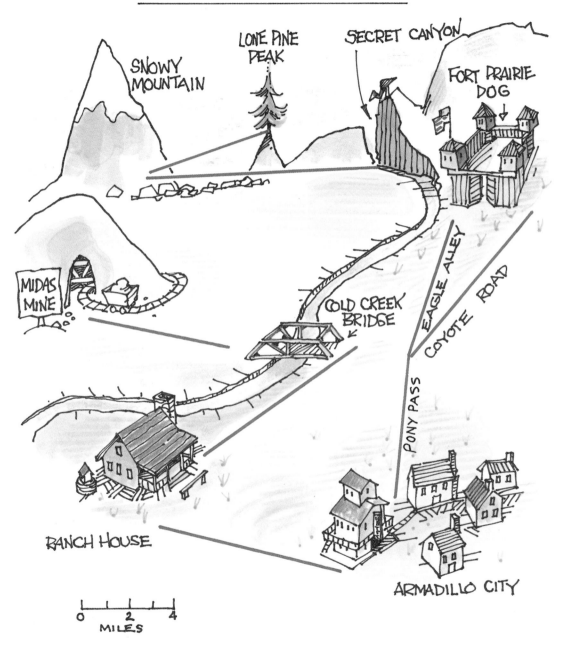

SNOWY MOUNTAIN

LONE PINE PEAK

SECRET CANYON

FORT PRAIRIE DOG

MIDAS MINE

COLD CREEK BRIDGE

EAGLE ALLEY

COYOTE ROAD

PONY PASS

RANCH HOUSE

ARMADILLO CITY

0   2   4
MILES

Elevation tells how high above sea level a place is.

Color It Blue

Because land isn't always flat, mapmakers need ways to show elevation. One way they do this is with color. The color key on a map tells you what elevation the map colors stand for.

Look at the map of Goat Mountain on page 9. What elevation level does the color green stand for? What color represents 18,000 feet (5,490 meters)?

Race a friend to the top of Goat Mountain.

- First, cut 8 strips of heavy paper about this size:

Sea level is the height of the ocean where it meets the land. Sea level is zero elevation.

- Color one strip white. Then, color one strip to match each color on the elevation bar. (Color one side of the paper only.)

- Cut the strips in half and throw away one white strip. Put all the strips color side down and mix them up.

- Take turns picking elevation strips until one player has all the colors to reach the top of the mountain.

Important! You have to pick the colors in order from bottom to top. If you pick a color out of order, it goes back in the pile and you lose your turn.

The highest mountain in the world is Mt. Everest. It's 29,029 feet (8,850 meters) high.

KEY

18,000 ft. (5,490 m.)
10,000 ft. (3,050 m.)
6,000 ft. (1,830 m.)
3,000 ft. (910 m.)
1,000 ft. (300 m.)
600 ft. (180 m.)
300 ft. (90 m.)
SEA LEVEL

Danger: If you pick the white strip, you've been hit by an avalanche! Put all of the colors you've collected, and the avalanche strip, back in the pile and start your climb again.

Ring Around the Mountain

Contour lines show the land cut in slices.

Another way that mapmakers show the ups and downs of the land is by using contour lines. Each line connects land that is at the same elevation above sea level. The closer together the lines are, the steeper the ground is. Here is how a small rise in the land would look on a contour map:

A steep mountain would look like this:

 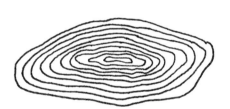

A hill that is sloping on one side and steep on the other would look like this:

You can make a contour map of a potato "mountain."

Cut part of a potato off so it will stand up. (You might need an adult to help you cut the potato.)

Next, cut the potato mountain into equal slices—1/4-inch slices, or a bit larger, should be okay. Keep the slices together.

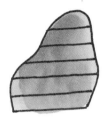

Take the bottom slice, place it on a piece of paper, and carefully draw around it with a sharp pencil. Set the slice aside.

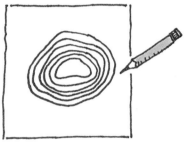

Take the next slice, and set it on top of the contour you just drew. Don't worry if it's the same size—it just means your mountain is steep. Draw around this slice, then stack it on the first one. Do this with each slice of your mountain.

Hint: If you wipe the slices with a paper towel, your drawing paper will stay drier.

When you're done, look at the contour map and the potato mountain. See what the lines tell about the shape of the mountain.

Bike Trip

It's a great day for a bike trip! Use the topographic map on the next page to help you plan your trip. It shows the elevation of the land, as well as where roads and towns are located.

- Which way would you go for the easiest ride?

- Where would you get the best workout on a mountain bike?

- Would it be harder to bike through Centerville or Spring Valley?

A topographic map shows both natural and human-made features.

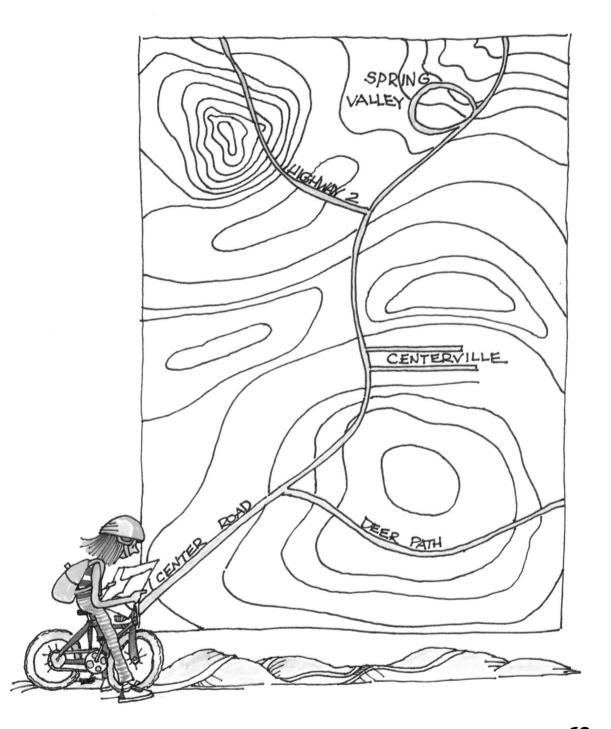

SPRING VALLEY

HIGHWAY 2

CENTERVILLE

CENTER ROAD

DEER PATH

13

Twisted Trip

Help Little Red Riding Hood plan her visit to Grandma's House. You will need:

- A length of string
- A ruler

Use the string to follow the twisty roads. Use the ruler to measure how much string it takes to get from one place to another. Check the scale bar to answer Red's questions about her trip.

- How many miles is it to Grandma's House if I take River Road? If I take Wolf Way?
- Will it take longer to go by Boulder Park or Sherwood Forest?
- How many kilometers would each route be?

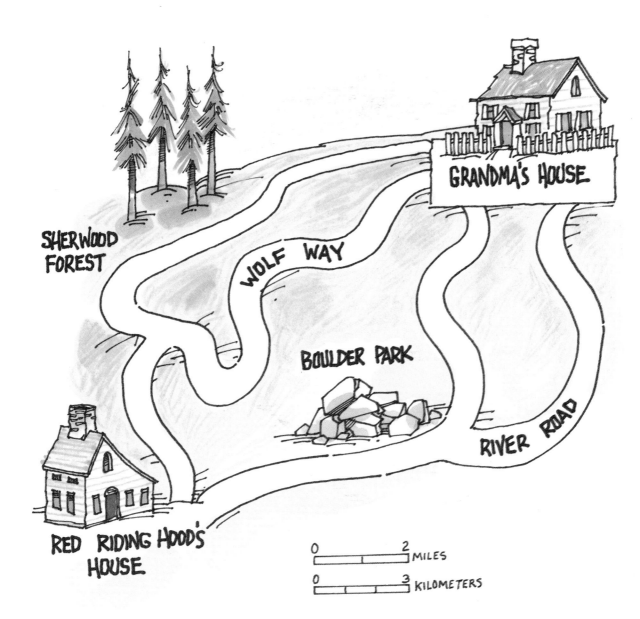

The altitude—or height—a pilot flies is measured in feet or meters.

You Be the Pilot

Study the map on the next page. Pretend you are taking tourists for a sightseeing trip in a small plane. You have several different tour routes you can take from the airport.

- How low can you fly without crashing into something on the City Skyline Tour?

- What tour would you take to get close to Deer Mountain if you fly at 3,000 feet (910 meters)?

- How high will you have to fly to take the Wilderness Valley Tour?

- If you are flying at 6,000 feet (1,830 meters), which mountains will you have to avoid?

Maps for pilots are called "charts."

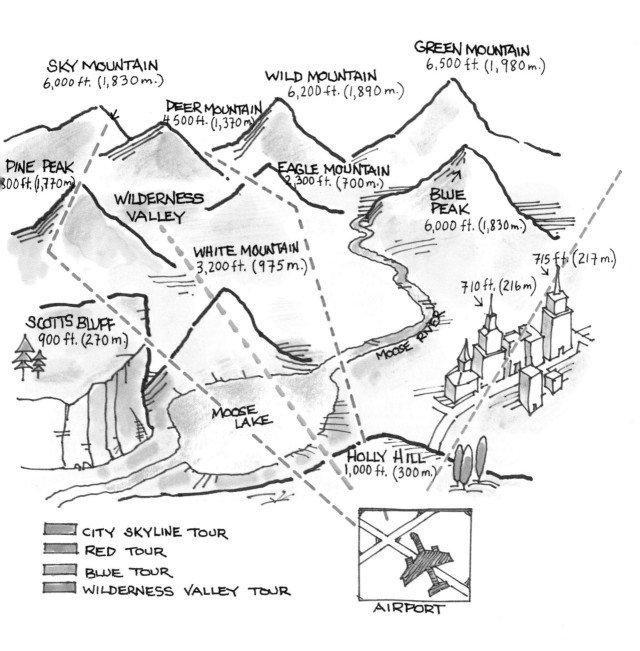

SKY MOUNTAIN
6,000 ft. (1,830 m.)

GREEN MOUNTAIN
6,500 ft. (1,980 m.)

WILD MOUNTAIN
6,200 ft. (1,890 m.)

DEER MOUNTAIN
4,500 ft. (1,370 m.)

PINE PEAK
800 ft. (1,770 m.)

EAGLE MOUNTAIN
2,300 ft. (700 m.)

BLUE PEAK
6,000 ft. (1,830 m.)

WILDERNESS VALLEY

WHITE MOUNTAIN
3,200 ft. (975 m.)

715 ft. (217 m.)

710 ft. (216 m.)

SCOTTS BLUFF
900 ft. (270 m.)

MOOSE RIVER

MOOSE LAKE

HOLLY HILL
1,000 ft. (300 m.)

CITY SKYLINE TOUR
RED TOUR
BLUE TOUR
WILDERNESS VALLEY TOUR

AIRPORT

17

Diving for Treasure

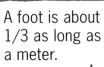

Depth used to be measured in fathoms.

Ready, set, DIVE! Go diving with a friend for sunken treasure. Since ocean depths can be measured in feet or meters, you'll have to do some figuring as you dive. To play, you'll need:

- One of a pair of dice, called a die
- Coins for markers
- A calculator to change feet to meters
- Six same-size pieces of paper, each marked with a different depth: 500 feet, 800 feet, 2,000 feet, 5,000 feet, 16,000 feet, and 25,000 feet.

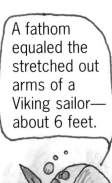

A fathom equaled the stretched out arms of a Viking sailor—about 6 feet.

How to play:

- Place your markers on START. Put the depth papers face down and mix them up. Take turns rolling the die to find out how many spaces to move.
- Follow the directions on the spaces.
- A CHANGE space means that you draw a depth paper, multiply the feet by 0.3 to get meters, and move to that space. Put the depth paper back in the pile.
- The TUMBLE INTO THE TRENCH space means that you need to roll a 5 to get back to the playing path. Continue diving on your next turn.
- The first player to reach the treasure wins!

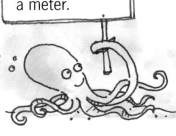

A foot is about 1/3 as long as a meter.

START

SPOT A STINGRAY GO AHEAD 2

TANGLED IN SEAWEED LOSE A TURN

CHANGE

50 M OUT OF AIR BACK TO START

SHARK CHASES YOU AHEAD 3

CHANGE

150 M TRANSFER TO DEEP-SEA SUB LOSE A TURN

SPERM WHALE THINKS YOU ARE DINNER AHEAD 4

600 M LOSE YOUR LIGHT BACK 3

UNDERSEA LAB

250 M GIANT SQUID ATTACK! BACK 2

1,500 M MOVE AHEAD 2

240 M

1,800 M

CHANGE

CHANGE

4,800 M PHOTOGRAPH RARE FISH AHEAD 2

STOP! ROLL 3 TO REACH TREASURE

OUT OF FILM BACK TO UNDERSEA LAB

7,500 M

CHANGE

TUMBLE INTO THE TRENCH

THIS IS THE DEEPEST SPOT IN ALL THE OCEANS

MARIANA TRENCH 36,198 FEET 11,033 METERS

19

Skateboard Scooting

In a city or town, a common way to measure distance is in blocks instead of miles. Imagine that you have hopped on your skateboard or bike, and are traveling around town using the map on the next page. Start and end at the X's—and be careful crossing the streets!

- How many blocks is it from the library to the Elm Street entrance of the swimming pool?

- Which is the shorter route between Pete's Pizza and the Ice Cream Shop—Elm Street and Maple Avenue, or Grant Street and Chase Road?

- You want to take a long time getting from home to school. Should you take Forest Avenue and Prairie Avenue? Or Forest Avenue, Maple Avenue, and Chase Road?

- Your friend tells you he took three streets to get from the video store to the bookstore. How many blocks did he travel?

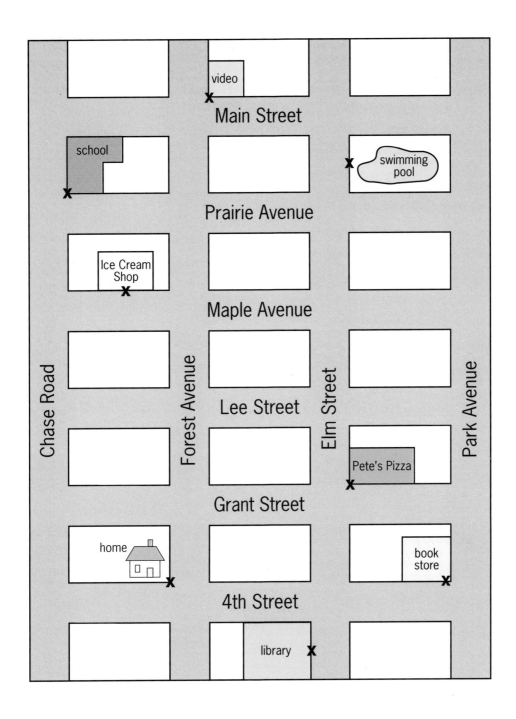

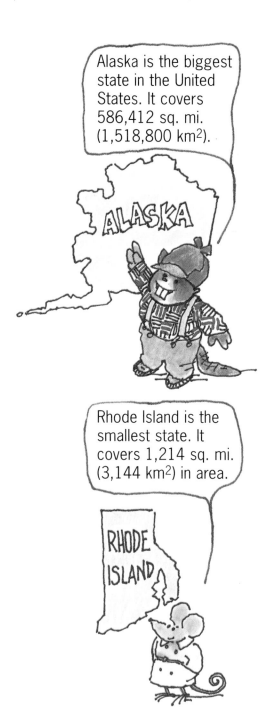

Alaska is the biggest state in the United States. It covers 586,412 sq. mi. (1,518,800 km²).

ALASKA

Rhode Island is the smallest state. It covers 1,214 sq. mi. (3,144 km²) in area.

RHODE ISLAND

City Planner

Square miles (sq. mi.) or square kilometers (km²) are used to measure the area that a city, county, or state covers. Call your city or town hall and find out the area in square miles of the city or town you live in. Do you think it is larger or smaller than the closest town to you?

Look at the map of Rodent County on the next page. Each square represents one square mile. Which city is the largest in area? How many square miles is it? What is the area of Hamster Heights? Is Mouseville or Beaver Bay 9 square miles? Which two cities are the same size?

Copy Gerbil Grove on a piece of graph paper. How many other ways could you shape this town and keep it the same area? (**Hint:** There are as many other shapes as there are square miles in Gerbil Grove.)

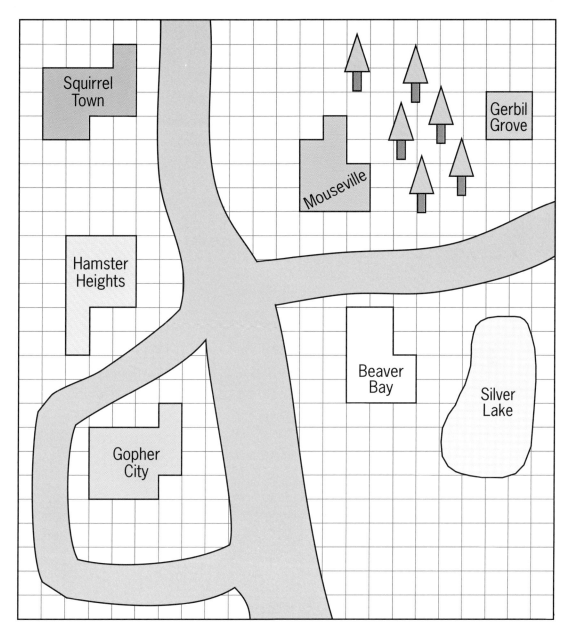

Rodent County

1 square mile = 2.59 square kilometers

There are 640 acres to a square mile and 100 hectares to a square kilometer.

Founder's Day

Join the pioneers who are heading west to claim land. If you get enough acres to make a square mile, you can found a town and choose a name for it. To play Founder's Day with a friend, you will need:

- One of a pair of dice
- Coins for markers
- Paper and pencils for keeping score

In the old days, an acre was the amount of land a pair of oxen could plow in one day.

How to play:

- Place your markers at START. Take turns rolling the die to find out how many spaces to move.

- Follow the directions on the spaces. Keep track of how many acres you collect.

- If you land on a LOSE ACRES space and you don't have enough acres to give up, your score goes back to zero.

- The first person to collect 640 (or more) acres moves directly to the Land Office to get a town WELCOME sign and win the game. Don't forget to choose a name for your town!

A Corny Puzzle

Farmer Jack has 30 pigs and Farmer Jill has 20 pigs. Jack's farm uses 90 square acres of corn to feed his pigs. Jill's farm uses 60 square acres of corn to feed hers. The brown areas are planted with corn. Does this farm belong to Jack or Jill?

To find square acres, multiply the number of acres wide by the number of acres long.

Dialing for Distance

How far is it to the mall? The park? The library? If you go by car, you can tell by checking the odometer. It looks like this:

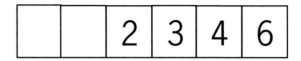

Make a chart like the one below. The next time you go somewhere in a car, write the numbers showing on the odometer at the start of the trip and the numbers showing at the end of the trip. (You can ignore the numbers in the last space on the right of the odometer.) Subtract the smaller number from the larger number to see how many miles you traveled. (If the numbers are the same, the trip was less than a mile.) Do this for trips to several different places.

TRIP	START	END	MILES TRAVELED
home to park	2346	2349	2349 − 2346 **3**
home to Mike's house	2377	2384	2384 − 2377 **7**

Think of other ways to get to the same places. Predict whether the new routes will be shorter or longer. Ask the driver to follow the routes you plotted. Keep track of the mileage to see if you are right.

Answers

P. 4, Pace It Off

The maps would not look the same because they are not using the same unit of measurement. For example, the bedroom map will show more "kid feet" between the door and the bed, and less "grown-up feet."

P. 5, Large-Scale: Small-Scale

B D C A

Pps. 6–7, Near and Far

It is 10 miles from Snowy Mountain to Secret Canyon. Cold Creek Bridge to the Ranch House is a greater distance (about 8 miles) than Midas Mine to Cold Creek Bridge (about 6 miles). It is 14 miles if you take Coyote Road to Pony Pass. It is 12 miles if you take Eagle Alley to Pony Pass. It is 8 miles from the Ranch House to Armadillo City.

Pps. 8–9, Color It Blue

6,000 feet (1,830 meters). Blue.

Pps. 10–11, Ring Around the Mountain

No answers.

Pps. 12–13, Bike Trip

The easiest ride would be Center Road and Deer Path. Because the contour lines are fairly far apart, you know the land will not be very hilly.

You'll really have to pump to travel Highway 2! The close contour lines mean steep land—a great trip for a mountain bike!

Centerville is located between two widely-spaced elevation lines, so it would be pretty easy biking. Spring Valley would be more hilly, since it lies across three different elevations.

Pps. 14–15, Twisted Trip

River Road and Wolf Way are both about 13 miles from Red Riding Hood's house.

It will take longer to go by Sherwood Forest (12 miles) than by Boulder Park (11 miles).

Going by Sherwood Forest would be a little more than 18 kilometers; Wolf Way would be 19.5 kilometers; going by Boulder Park would be 16.5 kilometers; and River Road would be 19.5 kilometers.

29

Pps. 16–17, You Be the Pilot

You won't crash into anything on the City Skyline Tour if you fly at an altitude of at least 716 feet (218 meters).

If you're flying at 3,000 feet (910 meters), you'll want to take the Blue Tour to Deer Mountain. If you took the Red Tour, you wouldn't be able to get over 5,800-foot (1,770-meter) Pine Peak.

On the Wilderness Valley Tour, you will have to fly at an altitude of at least 3,201 feet (976 meters) to get over White Mountain.

If you are flying at 6,000 feet, you will not be able to go over Blue Peak (6,000 ft. [1,830 meters]), Sky Mountain (6,000 ft. [1,830 meters]), Wild Mountain (6,200 ft. [1,890 meters]), or Green Mountain (6,500 ft. [1,980 meters]).

Pps. 18–19, Diving for Treasure

No answers.

Pps. 20–21, Skateboard Scooting

It is 5 blocks from the library to the Elm Street entrance of the swimming pool.

If you are going from Pete's Pizza to the Ice Cream Shop, it is shorter to go by Elm Street and Maple Avenue (3 1/2 blocks) than to go by Grant Street and Chase Road (4 1/2 blocks).

Which way to go from home to school? It doesn't matter—both are 5 blocks long!

If your friend took three streets to the bookstore, he took Main Street to Elm Street to 4th Street—a total of 7 blocks.

Pps. 22–23, City Planner

Different real cities and towns will have different areas.

As for Rodent County, Gopher City has the largest area—12 square miles (31 sq. km); the area of Hamster Heights is 11 square miles (28 sq. km); Mouseville is 9 square miles (23 sq. km) (Beaver Bay is 10 square miles [26 sq. km]); and Squirrel Town and Hamster Heights are the same size— 11 square miles (28 sq. km).

Gerbil Grove can be shaped in these other ways and still be 4 square miles (10 sq. km) in area:

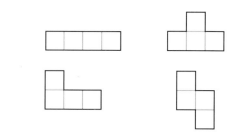

Pps. 24–25, Founder's Day

No answers.

P. 26, A Corny Puzzle

There are 60 square acres, so the farm belongs to Farmer Jill.
3x6 = 18, 2x4 = 8, 2x7 = 14, 5x4 = 20 (18 + 8 + 14 + 20 = 60)

P. 28, Dialing for Distance

Everyone's chart will differ.

Glossary

acre A unit of area. There are 640 acres in a square mile.

altitude Height above sea level.

chart A map used by airline and ship pilots.

contour line A line connecting points that are the same elevation above sea level. Mapmakers use contour lines to show the ups and downs of the land.

elevation How high above sea level a place is.

hectare A metric unit of area. One hectare equals about 2 1/2 acres.

kilometer A metric unit of distance. One kilometer equals a little more than 1 1/2 miles.

large-scale map A large-scale map shows a small area, with a lot of detail.

mile A unit of distance. One mile equals 5,280 feet.

sea level The height of the ocean where it meets the land. Sea level is zero elevation.

small-scale map A small-scale map shows a large area, with very little detail.

topographic map A map showing both natural and human-made features. It gives a true picture of what an area looks like.

Index